Contents

Today

Today, you have a toilet in your house. When you flush it, it empties into sewers underground.

900 years ago

700 years ago

500 years ago

But it was not
always like that.

	300 **years ago**		**100** **years ago**	**Today**

3

9oo years ago

Long ago, some people lived in castles. There were toilets inside the castle that emptied into the moat outside.

900 years ago

700 years ago

500 years ag

4

The moat became very smelly when the weather was hot.

300
years ago

100
years ago

Today

5

500 years ago

For hundreds of years most people did not have a toilet in the house.

900
years ago

700
years ago

500
years ag

The toilet was built outside and was shared by lots of other people.

300
years ago

100
years ago

Today

7

At night a chamber pot was used in the house.
In the morning it was emptied out of the
bedroom window into the street.

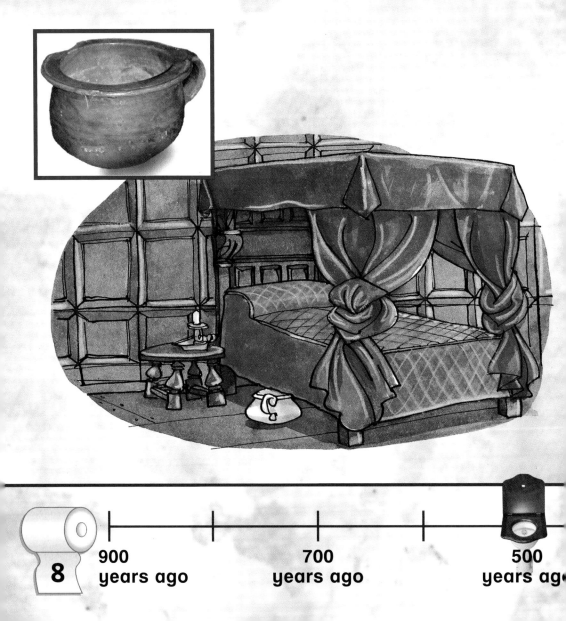

900
years ago

700
years ago

500
years ag

When people did this, they shouted 'Watch out for the water!' so that anyone below could try to get out of the way in time.

300
years ago

100
years ago

Today

300 years ago

The outside toilet was just a big hole in the ground, with a seat over it.

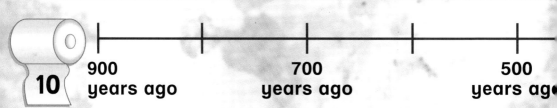

When the hole was full, men came to dig it out. They did this at night because the smell was so bad.

300
years ago

100
years ago

Today

They took the waste away in a cart. Sometimes they took it to dunghills outside the town, but often they threw it in the river.

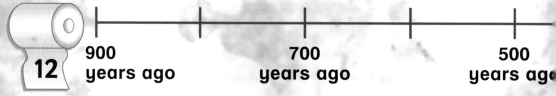

900 years ago

700 years ago

500 years ago

300
years ago

100
years ago

Today

13

The water that was used for cooking, washing and drinking also came from the river.

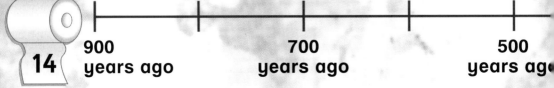

900
years ago

700
years ago

500
years ag

Thousands of people became ill and died because they had been drinking dirty water.

300
years ago

100
years ago

Today

100 years ago

In the 1880s, a man called Thomas Crapper invented a flush toilet that worked properly.

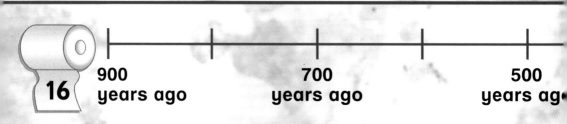

900 years ago   700 years ago   500 years ago

A tradtional Crapper flushing toilet.

Thomas Crapper & Co.

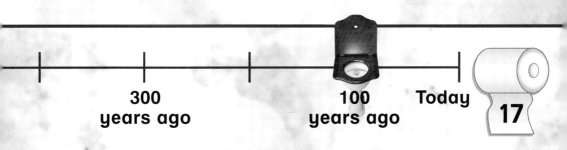

300 years ago

100 years ago

Today

17

After that, more and more people began to
have flush toilets fitted inside their houses.

Nowadays, all modern homes have flush toilets.

A modern flushing toilet.

Toilets in the past

"The first toilet on a train was made
for Queen Victoria in 1840."

"In one part of Leeds in 1839, 452 people had to
share just two outside privies."

Thomas Crapper & Co.

"When it was first invented, toilet paper was a luxury. Most people tore newspaper into little squares and used that instead."

"For many years during the 1900s everyone had to pay one penny to use a public toilet. Today, some people still say they are going 'to spend a penny'."

Glossary

chamber pot   large china bowl with a handle

dunghill   a large rubbish tip

moat   a ditch filled with water around the outside of a castle

privies   old word for toilets

sewers   large pipes that carry water and waste to a sewage works